OFFICE FUN!

By

Paul E. Bierley

With kindest regards to my fellow Rockwell musician, Bill Maurer,

Paul E. Bierley
24 August 1977

INTEGRITY PRESS   Cartoon Series

Published by
INTEGRITY PRESS
3888 Morse Road
Columbus, Ohio 43219

First Printing October, 1976

Library of Congress Number 76-39578
ISBN 0-918048-01-X

Composition and Printing By
MID-AMERICAN GRAPHICS
WESTERVILLE, OHIO

FOREWORD
Or, in this case,
FORECARTOON

If at times you've wished the office goldbrick would get his come-uppance, you and I might have something in common. If there have been times when you were certain your boss was something less than perfect or you felt that management was insensitive to your well being, then I'm *sure* of it.

But perhaps we are different in that I let off steam by adding an element of satire to trying situations. This way I don't get gray hairs or ulcers, you see.

I give them, however! My cartoons have made me both popular and unpopular at the same time, particularly in management circles, where I've "plowed too close to the corn." I love it.

If you haven't seen my cartoons in trade journals recently, it's because I have been busy on some long overdue literary efforts. As the biographer of John Philip Sousa, I was obliged to complete several books and articles in time for the Bicentennial.

I'm not weary of writing biographies, but after such serious endeavors I've had a very strong urge to exercise my funnybone again. This set of cartoons is the result, and all I did was reach into an ever-growing pile of rough sketches, polish them up and try them on several dozen office workers. From over 400 cartoons, these 100 emerged as the ones most likely to strike responsive chords.

John Philip Sousa often said he'd rather be the composer of an inspired march than the composer of a manufactured symphony. Paraphrasing this, let me say that I would rather be the originator of an inspired cartoon than the assembler of manufactured humor in any form. I am proud of the fact that each cartoon in this volume was inspired by an incident from my own experience.

Hopefully you'll see yourself in these pages. If you find yourself in a predicament which seems unbearable, try to imagine how humorous it might seem to others. Then you're walking in my shoes. If you identify with my not-so-imaginary characters and see the humor of it all, you will have made my day.

The chances are that despite how bad your situation seems, you'll be bragging about it to your grandchildren — and chuckling. In the words of one of the cartoons, "In twenty years they'll be calling these the 'good old days.'"

Paul E. Bierley

"I see you've graduated from eating coins."

"Odd man buys!"

"The way you study anatomy, Stauffer, you should be in medical school."

"I thought you were a big shot until I saw how low your wall is."

"No, I'm not financially independent; I'm financially contemptuous."

"Sure, I'm slow, but have you noticed how quiet I am?"

"Would you hit this apple a lick? I'm going in to see the boss."

"I've completed the evaluation of your management improvement plan, Asmus."

"Hurry it up!"

"I'd like a metric scale 11.8110 inches long."

"You're a good man, Hyde. You can think of more things that won't work than anybody else."

"Wake up, Sackinger. It's quitting time."

"Boss, we made BUSINESS WEEK!"

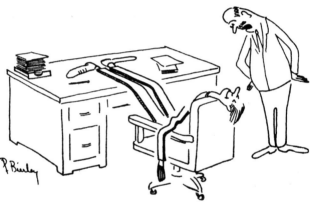

"I know the doctor told you to relax more, but
this is ridiculous."

"Stupid reorganization, eh, buddy?"

"I mean...SIR?"

" . . . And this is my private conference room."

"That's 'Go to hell, SIR'!"

"Now see here, Mr. Simms! Just because you worked until midnight last night that doesn't entitle you to come in late the next morning!"

"The boss lives just to find fault with my drawings!"

"Seven bucks an hour he's gettin'!"

"Well, you asked for it."

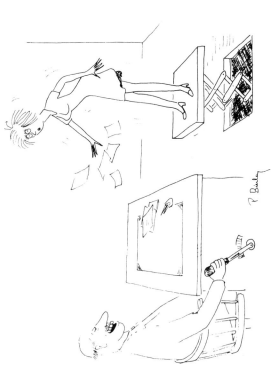

"Now about that raise you wanted, Miss Wallace . . ."

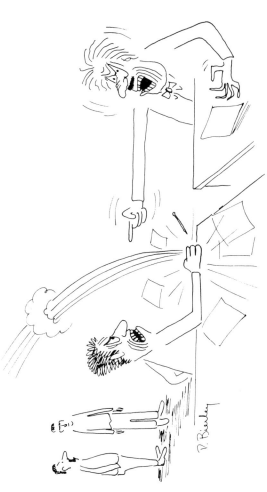

"They're arguing over whose boss is the stupidest."

"Air mail for you."

"Poor loser!"

"I suppose you think sales managers are a dime a dozen."

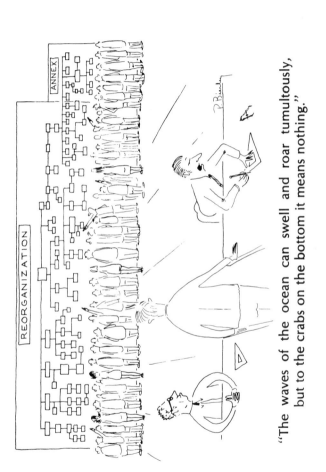

"The waves of the ocean can swell and roar tumultously, but to the crabs on the bottom it means nothing."

"If I knew exactly what had irritated him, I'd do more of it."

"Oh! Was that your coffee?"

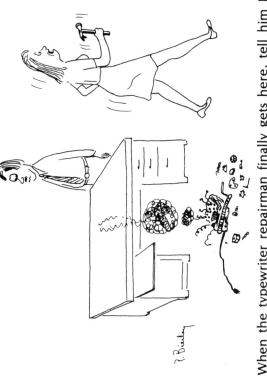

"When the typewriter repairman finally gets here, tell him I made the adjustment myself."

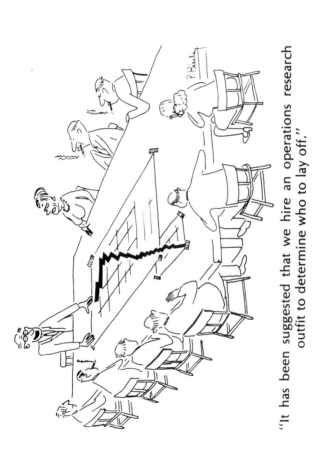

"It has been suggested that we hire an operations research outfit to determine who to lay off."

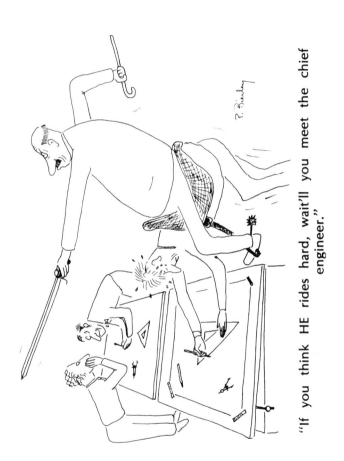

"If you think HE rides hard, wait'll you meet the chief engineer."

"I hear there's going to be a reorganization — esteemed, most honorable potential boss, sir."

"If you didn't have hands, Fuller, you couldn't talk!"

"What was the name of that fellow who taught us that memory course?"

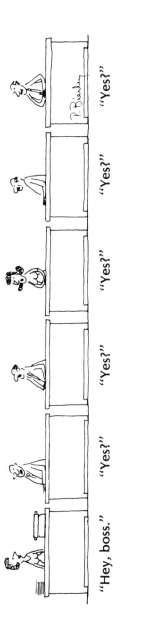

"Hail, hail, the gang's not all here!"

"Hurry up and finish this job so we can put you on layoff!"

"To get an idea about how fast you should move around, I want you to read up on glaciers."

"It's supposed to be DEVELOPMENT, but it's more correct this way."

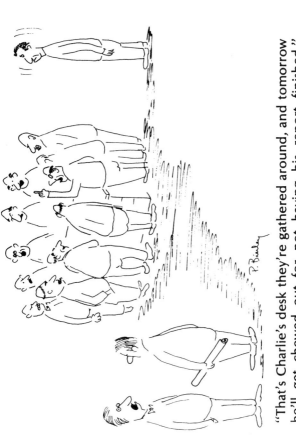

"That's Charlie's desk they're gathered around, and tomorrow he'll get chewed out for not having his report finished."

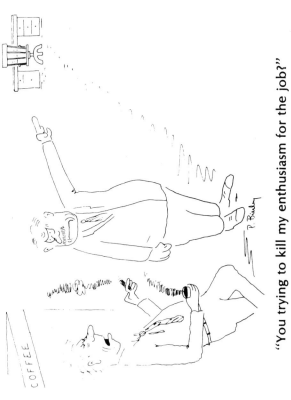

"You trying to kill my enthusiasm for the job?"

"You're a nice boss, Mr. Crump — in spite of what everybody says."

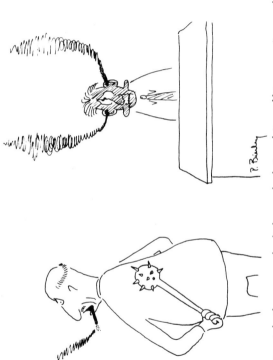

"If I catch the guy who's been helping himself to my cigars..."

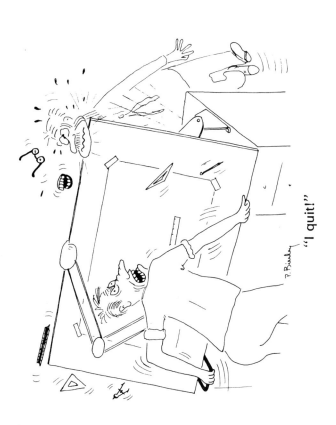

"I quit!"

P. Bunday

"So you didn't win first at the beauty contest — what's wrong with the BOOBY prize?"

P. Brinkley

"Better three hours too early than three minutes too late, so I'm leaving three hours early!"

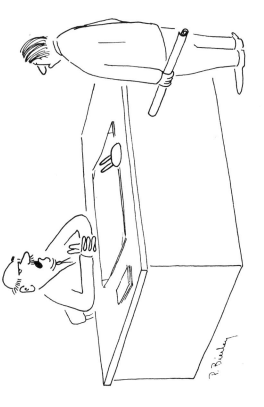

"You're just not management material, Stevens. You have too many ideas about how to improve working conditions."

"It's Ms. Longnecker. She's sensitive about losing her private office."

"Mr. Bailey had a stroke of genius, and the boss had a stroke!"

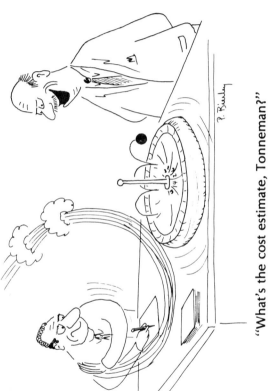

"What's the cost estimate, Tonneman?"

"We're on the verge of a technological breakthrough; we're on thin ice."

"Yessir, Moose has revolutionized snoring."

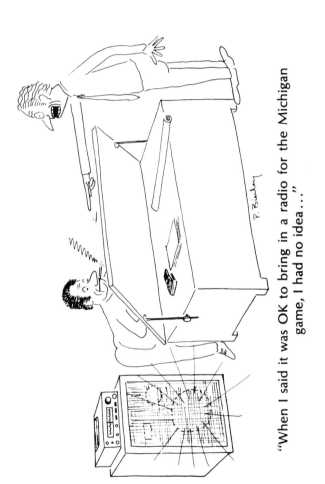

"When I said it was OK to bring in a radio for the Michigan game, I had no idea…"

P. Breuley

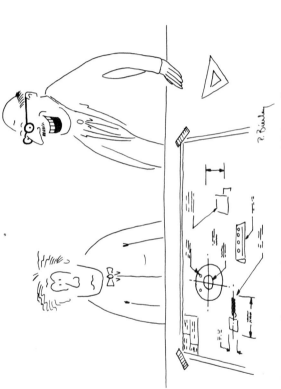

"Beautiful! A masterpiece of fakery!"

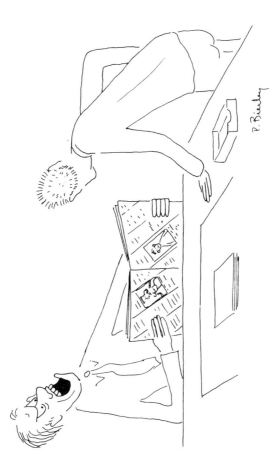

"The news in the company paper is always slanted!"

"I think we're headed in the right direction, but let's not go so far as to suggest that we're organized."

P. Birolay

"Joanie, we're out of these big clamps again."

"Where's the report?"

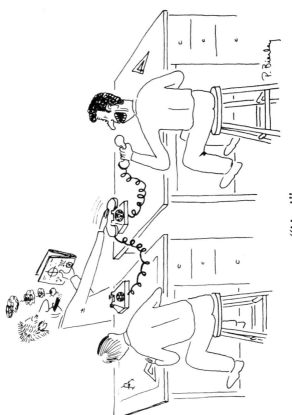

"Hey!"

"If all the world's aerodynamicists were laid end to end, they wouldn't reach a conclusion."

"They can't agree on points of disagreement."

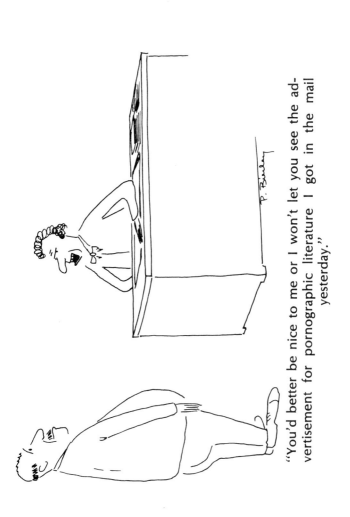

"You'd better be nice to me or I won't let you see the advertisement for pornographic literature I got in the mail yesterday."

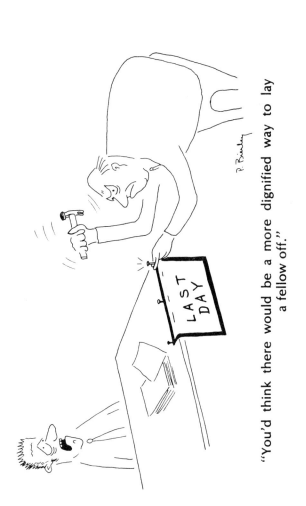

"You'd think there would be a more dignified way to lay a fellow off."

"No...on the CABINET."

"You do good work. Not much of it, but good."

"It all started with a friendly flip for coffee."

"I'm the new supervisor. What's your name?"

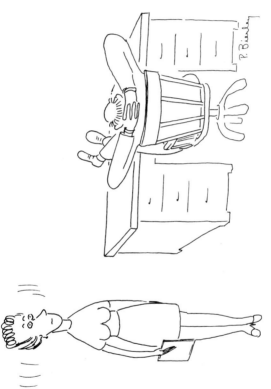

"I forgot something once, but I can't remember what it was."

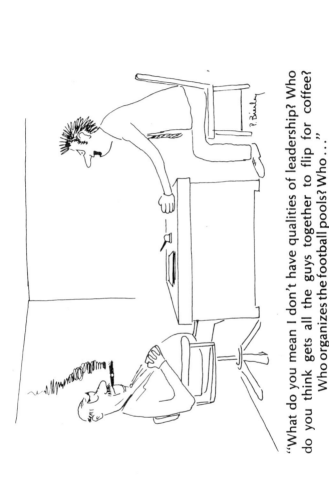

"What do you mean I don't have qualities of leadership? Who do you think gets all the guys together to flip for coffee? Who organizes the football pools? Who..."

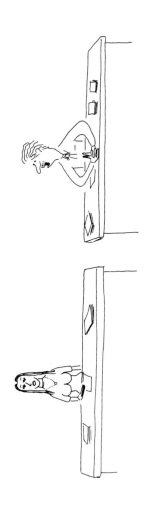

"We're in bad shape. My source for good rumors just got laid off."

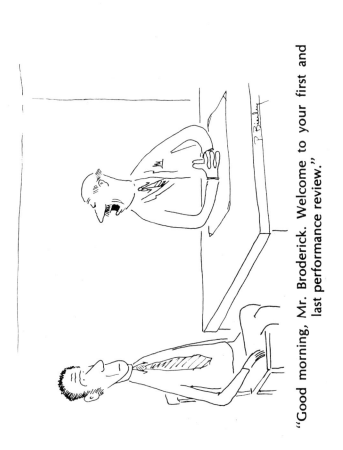

"Good morning, Mr. Broderick. Welcome to your first and last performance review."

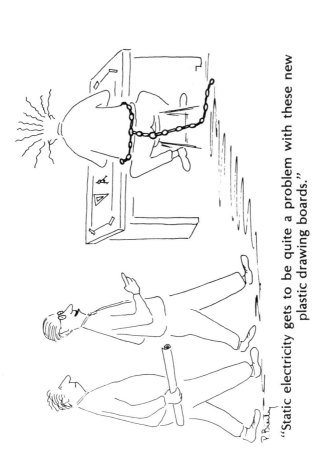

"Static electricity gets to be quite a problem with these new plastic drawing boards."

"That does it! From now on I'm eating out!"

"I was going to tell you a joke, but I remembered that you were the one who told it to me."

"Thanks for your opinion, Edith. The slave's point of view interests me."

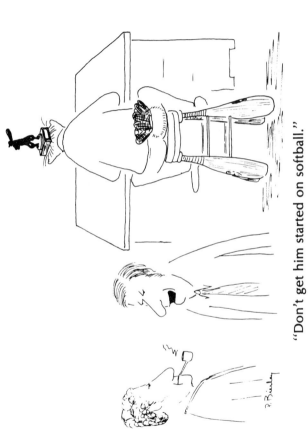

"Don't get him started on softball."

"What did you buy with your overtime check?"

"I didn't say 'mistake.' I said 'technical oversight.'"

"Charge!"

"Can you keep a secret?"

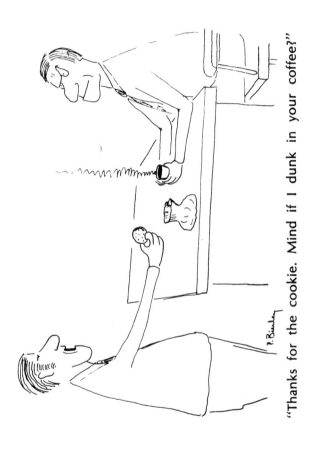

"Thanks for the cookie. Mind if I dunk in your coffee?"

"I hear they're getting rid of deadwood."

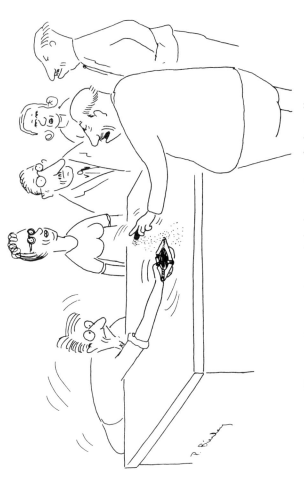

"I want the employees' desks neat and clean."

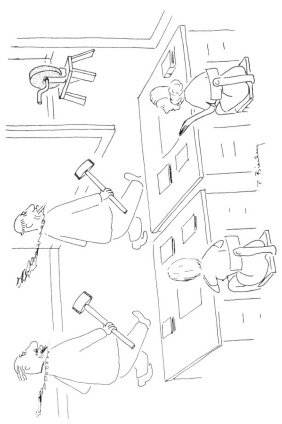

"I wonder what they're up to."

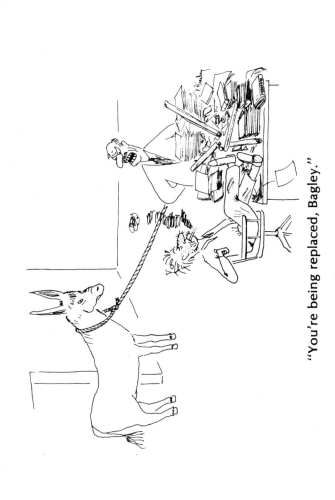

"You're being replaced, Bagley."

"Austerity's really taking hold around here!"

"Your wife's lunches really pack a whallop!"

"The way you get transferred from department to department, you should put wheels on your drafting machine."

"In twenty years they'll be calling these the 'good old days'."

"I'm worried, J.B. We haven't reorganized for over three weeks."

"I think I'll get my wife a subscription to PLAYBOY for Mother's Day."

"Old man Smith ought to retire."

"That settles it. We lay off Burns, Brown and Jackson."

"Wessell would rather have his teeth pulled than change his design."

"Ever see Waldorf do his famous double snap-roll?"

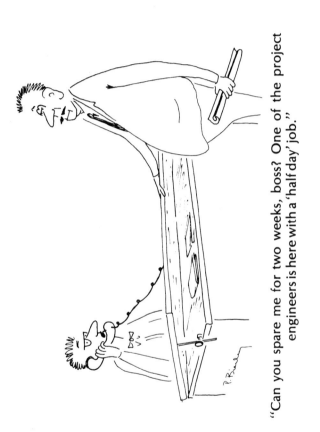

"Can you spare me for two weeks, boss? One of the project engineers is here with a 'half day' job."

"After all the apple-polishing he was doing, he was bound to get ahead in the world."

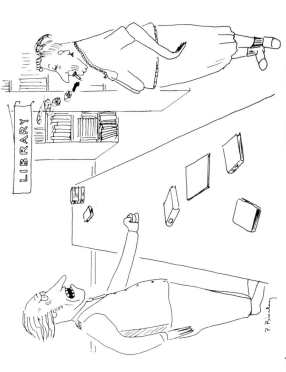

"Why was my report put in the RARE BOOKS section?"

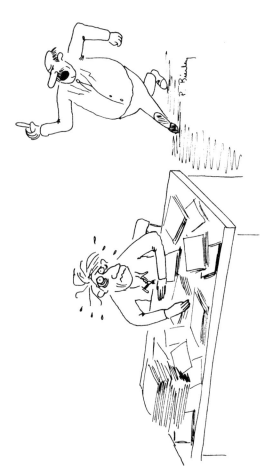

"Hold it! Everything's changed except the deadline!"